D1602092

MOMENTS BRIGHT AND SHINING

365
THOUGHTS TO ENJOY
DAY BY DAY

SELECTED BY PETER SEYMOUR

Published by
THE C.R. GIBSON COMPANY
Norwalk, Connecticut

A flower unblown; a book unread;
A tree with fruit unharvested;
A path untrod; a house whose rooms
Lack yet the heart's divine perfumes;
A landscape whose wide border lies
In silent shade beneath the skies;
A wondrous fountain yet unsealed;
A casket with its gifts concealed —
This is the Year that for you waits
Beyond tomorrow's mystic gates.

HORATIO NELSON POWERS

1

Even while we sing, he smiles his last,
And leaves our sphere behind.
The good Old Year is with the past,
O be the New as kind!

WILLIAM CULLEN BRYANT

 2

I do the very best I know how — the very best I can;
and I mean to keep doing so until the end. If the
end brings me out all right, what is said against me
won't amount to anything. If the end brings me out
wrong, ten angels swearing I was right would make
no difference.

ABRAHAM LINCOLN

 3

If men, with minds as cool as the evening, will lay
out the work of the day, they will be able, in this
leisurely January month, to lay plans for a life of
prosperity and happiness.

FARMER'S ALMANAC

 4

Oh! the snow, the beautiful snow,
Filling the sky and the earth below!
Over the housetops, over the street,
Over the heads of the people you meet:
    Dancing,
        Flirting,
            Skimming along.
Beautiful snow! it can do nothing wrong.

JOHN WHITTAKER WATSON

5 There is surely a piece of divinity in us, something that was before the elements, and owes no homage unto the sun.

SIR THOMAS BROWNE

 6 The map of America is a map of endlessness, of opening out, of forever and ever. No man's face would make you think of it but his hope might, his courage might.

ARCHIBALD MacLEISH

 7 To see a world in a grain of sand
And a heaven in a wild flower:
Hold infinity in the palm of your hand,
And eternity in an hour.

WILLIAM BLAKE

 8 There are but two roads that lead to an important goal and to the doing of great things: strength and perseverance. Strength is the lot but of a few privileged men; but austere perseverance, harsh and continuous, may be employed by the smallest of us and rarely fails of its purpose, for its silent power grows irresistibly greater with time.

JOHANN WOLFGANG VON GOETHE

 9 The safest way to double your money is to fold it over once and put it in your pocket.

KIN HUBBARD

 **10** Everyone wants to understand art. Why not try to understand the song of a bird? Why does one love the night, flowers, everything around one, without trying to understand them?

PABLO PICASSO

 **11** There are one-story intellects, two-story intellects, and three-story intellects with skylights. All fact collectors, who have no aim beyond their facts, are one-story men. Two-story men compare, reason, generalize, using the labors of the fact collectors as well as their own. Three-story men idealize, imagine, predict; their best illumination comes from above, through the skylight.

OLIVER WENDELL HOLMES

 **12** These are the gifts I ask
Of Thee, Spirit serene:
Strength for the daily task,
Courage to face the road,
Good cheer to help me bear the traveler's load,
And, for the hours of rest that come between,
An inward joy of all things heard and seen.

HENRY VAN DYKE

 **13** If you have an important point to make, don't try to be subtle or clever. Use a pile driver. Hit the point once. Then come back and hit it again. Then hit it a third time — a tremendous whack.

WINSTON CHURCHILL

 **14**

I believe that man will not merely endure: he will prevail. He is immortal, not because he alone among creatures has an inexhaustible voice, but because he has a soul, a spirit capable of compassion and sacrifice and endurance.

WILLIAM FAULKNER

 **15**

If you have known how to compose your life, you have done a great deal more than the man who knows how to compose a book. You have done more than the man who has taken cities and empires.

MICHEL DE MONTAIGNE

 **16**

Sweet are the uses of adversity,
Which, like the toad, ugly and venomous,
Wears yet a precious jewel in his head;
And this our life, exempt from public haunt,
Finds tongues in trees, books in the running brooks,
Sermons in stones, and good in every thing.
I would not change it.

WILLIAM SHAKESPEARE

 **17**

At bottom every man knows well-enough that he is a unique being, only once on this earth; and by no extraordinary chance will such a marvelously picturesque piece of diversity in unity as he is, ever be put together a second time.

FRIEDRICH NIETZSCHE

 **18** According to the Spanish proverb, four persons are wanted to make a good salad: a spendthrift for oil, a miser for vinegar, a counsellor for salt, and a madman to stir it all up.

ABRAHAM HAYWARD

 **19** A man reveals his character even in the simplest thing he does. A fool does not enter a room, nor leave it, nor sit down, nor rise, nor is he silent, nor does he stand up, like a man of sense and understanding.

JEAN DE LA BRUYÈRE

 **20** The especial genius of women I believe to be electrical in movement, intuitive in function, spiritual in tendency.

MARGARET FULLER

 **21** So long as we love, we serve; so long as we are loved by others, I would almost say that we are indispensable; and no man is useless while he has a friend.

ROBERT LOUIS STEVENSON

 **22** The worst sin towards our fellow creatures is not to hate them, but to be indifferent to them: that's the essence of inhumanity.

GEORGE BERNARD SHAW

 **23**
There is a tendency among many shallow thinkers
of our day to teach that every human act is a reflex,
over which we do not exercise human control. They
would rate a generous deed as no more praiseworthy
than a wink, a crime as no more voluntary than
a sneeze . . . Such a philosophy undercuts all human
dignity . . . All of us have the power of choice in
action at every moment of our lives.

FULTON J. SHEEN

 **24**
The only gracious way to accept an insult is
to ignore it; if you can't ignore it, top it; if you
can't top it, laugh at it; if you can't laugh at
it, it's probably deserved.

RUSSELL LYNES

 **25**
Anyone who stops learning is old, whether at twenty
or eighty. Anyone who keeps learning stays young.
The greatest thing in life is to keep your mind young.

HENRY FORD

 **26**
Enthusiasm is the element of success
in everything. It is the light that leads and the
strength that lifts men on and up in the great
struggles of scientific pursuits and of professional
labor. It robs endurance of difficulty, and makes
pleasure of duty.

BISHOP DOANE

 **27**
There is a spectacle more grand than the sea; it is
heaven; there is a spectacle more grand than
heaven; it is the conscience.

VICTOR HUGO

 **28**

There are loyal hearts, there are spirits brave,
　There are souls that are pure and true;
Then give to the world the best you have,
　And the best will come back to you.

MADELEINE BRIDGES

 **29**

Though it is but by footsteps ye do it,
　And hardships may hinder and stay;
Walk with faith, and be sure you'll get through it;
　For "Where there's a will there's a way."

ELIZA COOK

 **30**

True eloquence does not consist in speech.
Words and phrases may be marshalled
in every way, but they cannot compass it.
It must consist in the man, in the subject,
and in the occasion. It comes, if it comes at
all, like the outbreaking of a fountain from
the earth, or the bursting forth of volcanic
fires, with spontaneous, original,
native force.

DANIEL WEBSTER

 **31**

Not by appointment do we meet delight
Or joy; they heed not our expectancy;
But round some corner of the streets of life
They of a sudden greet us with a smile.

GERALD MASSEY

FEBRUARY

 1

Sleep, my child, and peace attend thee,
   All through the night;
Guardian angels God will lend thee,
   All through the night;
Soft the drowsy hours are creeping,
Hill and dale in slumber steeping,
Love alone his watch is keeping —
   All through the night.

OLD WELSH AIR

 2

The best compliment to a child or a friend is
the feeling you give him that he has been set free
to make his own inquiries, to come to conclusions
that are right for him, whether or not they
coincide with your own.

ALISTAIR COOKE

 **3**

You wouldn't say an ax handle has style to it.
It has beauty, and appropriateness of form, and a
"this-is-how-it-should-be-ness." But it has no style
because it has no mistakes. Style reflects one's
idiosyncrasies. Your personality is apt to show more
to the degree that you did not solve the problem
than to the degree that you did.

CHARLES EAMES

 4

The heart hath its own memory, like the mind,
   And in it are enshrined
The precious keepsakes, into which is wrought
   The giver's loving thought.

HENRY WADSWORTH LONGFELLOW

5 If you achieve success, you will get applause, and if you get applause, you will hear it. My advice to you concerning applause is this: Enjoy it but never quite believe it.

ROBERT MONTGOMERY

 6
Better never trouble Trouble
Until Trouble troubles you;
For you only make your trouble
Double-trouble when you do;
And the trouble — like a bubble —
That you're troubling about,
May be nothing but a cipher
With its rim rubbed out.

DAVID KEPPEL

 7 To endure is greater than to dare; to tire out hostile fortune; to be daunted by no difficulty; to keep heart when all have lost it; to go through intrigue spotless; to forego even ambition when the end is gained — who can say this is not greatness?

WILLIAM MAKEPEACE THACKERAY

 8 Affirmation of life is the spiritual act by which man ceases to live unreflectively and begins to devote himself to his life with reverence in order to raise it to its true value. To affirm life is to deepen, to make more inward, and to exalt the will-to-live.

ALBERT SCHWEITZER

9

We see then how far the monuments of wit and learning are more durable than the monuments of power, or of the hands. For have not the verses of Homer continued twenty-five hundred years, or more, without the loss of a syllable or letter; during which time infinite palaces, temples, castles, cities have been decayed and demolished?

FRANCIS BACON

 **10**

All things journey: sun and moon,
  Morning, noon, and afternoon,
    Night and all her stars;
Twixt the east and western bars
Round they journey,
  Come and go!
We go with them!

GEORGE ELIOT

 **11**

Courage is the best gift of all; courage stands before everything. It is what preserves our liberty, safety, life, and our homes and parents, our country and our children. Courage comprises all things: a man with courage has every blessing.

PLAUTUS

 **12**

I am not bound to win but I am bound to be true. I am not bound to succeed but I am bound to live up to what light I have. I must stand with anybody that stands right; stand with him while he is right and part with him when he goes wrong.

ABRAHAM LINCOLN

 **13** Brotherhood is not just a Bible word. Out of comradeship can come and will come the happy life for all. The underdog can and will lick his weight in the wildcats of the world.

HEYWOOD BROUN

 **14** To love very much is to love inadequately; we love — that is all. Love cannot be modified without being nullified. Love is a short word but it contains everything. Love means the body, the soul, the life, the entire being. We feel love as we feel the warmth of our blood, we breathe love as we breathe the air, we hold it in ourselves as we hold our thoughts. Nothing more exists for us. Love is not a word; it is a wordless state indicated by four letters . . .

GUY DE MAUPASSANT

 **15** But Oh, those heavenly moments when I feel this three-dimensional universe too small to contain my Attributes; when a sense of the divine Ipseity invades me; when I know that my voice is the voice of Truth, and my umbrella God's umbrella!

LOGAN PEARSALL SMITH

 **16** The secret of happiness is this: Let your interests be as wide as possible, and let your reactions to the things and persons that interest you be as far as possible friendly rather than hostile.

BERTRAND RUSSELL

 **17** The rung of a ladder was never meant to rest upon, but only to hold a man's foot long enough to enable him to put the other somewhat higher.

THOMAS HENRY HUXLEY

 **18** Silence is the element in which great things fashion themselves together; that at length they may emerge, full-formed and majestic, into the daylight of Life, which they are thenceforth to rule.

THOMAS CARLYLE

 **19** If you your lips would keep from slips,
Five things observe with care:
Of whom you speak, to whom you speak,
And how and when and where.

If you your ears would save from jeers,
These things keep mildly hid:
Myself and I, and mine and my,
And how I do and did.

AUTHOR UNKNOWN

 **20** We should tell ourselves once and for all that it is the first duty of the soul to become as happy, complete, independent, and great as lies in its power.
To this end we may sacrifice even the passion for sacrifice, for sacrifice never should be the means of ennoblement, but only the sign of being ennobled.

MAURICE MAETERLINCK

 **21**

If a man can write a better book, preach a better sermon, or make a better mousetrap than his neighbors, though he builds his house in the woods, the world will make a beaten path to his door.

RALPH WALDO EMERSON

 **22**

America has furnished to the world the character of Washington. And if our American institutions have done nothing else, that alone would have entitled them to the respect of mankind.

DANIEL WEBSTER

 **23**

Without recognition of human rights, we shall never have peace; and it is only within the framework of peace that human rights can be fully developed. In fact, the work for peace is basically a work for the most elementary human right: the right of everyone to security and freedom from fear.

DAG HAMMARSKJÖLD

 **24**

Do all the good you can,
By all the means you can,
In all the ways you can,
In all the places you can,
At all the times you can,
To all the people you can,
As long as ever you can.

JOHN WESLEY

 **25**

Blessed are they who have the gift of making friends, for it is one of God's best gifts. It involves many things, but above all, the power of going out of one's self, and appreciating whatever is noble and loving in another.

THOMAS HUGHES

 **26**

O God, grant us the serenity to accept
What cannot be changed;
The courage to change what can be changed,
And the wisdom to know the one from the other.

REINHOLD NIEBUHR

 **27**

Giving comfort under affliction requires that penetration into the human mind, joined to that experience which knows how to soothe, how to reason, and how to ridicule, taking the utmost care not to apply those arts improperly.

HENRY FIELDING

 **28**

Hope, like the gleaming taper's light,
    Adorns and cheers our way;
And still, as darker grows the night,
    Emits a brighter ray.

OLIVER GOLDSMITH

 **29**

Ah, but a man's reach should exceed his grasp,
Or what's a heaven for?

ROBERT BROWNING

1

The Wind, so often sung about,
That whistles through the tree
And guides the course and destiny
Of ships upon the sea,
Will gladly blow your hat off for
A small, additional fee.

PHILIP LAZARUS

 2

For a few minutes every day practice quietness.
Choose a place where you can relax completely.
Quietness and silence are a healing balm for a tired
body and brain, frayed nerves, and needless
foreboding.

GRENVILLE KLEISER

 3

Six essential qualities that are the key to success:
Sincerity, personal integrity, humility, courtesy,
wisdom, charity.

WILLIAM MENNINGER

 4

It may well be doubted whether human ingenuity
can construct an enigma of the kind which human
ingenuity may not, by proper application resolve.

EDGAR ALLAN POE

 5

All creatures seek after unity; all multiplicity
struggles toward it — the universal aim of all life
is always this unity. All that flows outward is to
flow backward into its source — God.

JOHANN TAULER

6 The desert is the last place you can see all around you. The light out here makes everything close, and it is never, never the same. Sometimes the light hits the mountains from behind and front at the same time, and it gives them the look of Japanese prints, you know, distances in layers.

GEORGIA O'KEEFFE

 7 We sleep, but the loom of life never stops and the pattern which was weaving when the sun went down is weaving when it comes up to-morrow.

HENRY WARD BEECHER

 8 A thing of beauty is a joy forever:
Its loveliness increases; it will never
Pass into nothingness; but still will keep
A bower quiet for us, and a sleep
Full of sweet dreams, and health, and quiet breathing.

JOHN KEATS

 9 There are but two powers in the world, the sword and the mind. In the long run the sword is always beaten by the mind.

NAPOLEON BONAPARTE

 **10** Dare to be wise: begin! He who postpones the hour of living rightly is like the rustic who waits for the river to run out before he crosses, yet on it glides, and will glide forever.

HORACE

 **11**

A wise old owl sat on an oak,
The more he saw the less he spoke;
The less he spoke the more he heard;
Why aren't we like that wise old bird?

EDWARD HERSEY RICHARDS

 **12**

Adventure is something you seek for pleasure,
or even for profit, like a gold rush or invading a
country; for the illusion of being more alive than
ordinarily, the thing you *will* to occur; but
experience is what really happens to you in the
long run; the truth that finally overtakes you.

KATHERINE ANNE PORTER

 **13**

Politeness has been defined as love in trifles.
Courtesy is said to be love in little things.
And the one secret of politeness is to love.
Love cannot behave itself unseemly.

HENRY DRUMMOND

 **14**

And wouldn't it be nicer
    For you to smile than pout,
And so make sunshine in the house
    When there is none without?

PHOEBE CARY

 **15**

Walk on a rainbow trail; walk on a trail of song,
and all about you will be beauty. There is a way out
of every dark mist, over a rainbow trail.

NAVAJO SONG

 **16** The lessons of great men are lost unless they reinforce upon our minds the highest demands which we make upon ourselves; that they are lost unless they drive our sluggish wills forward in the direction of their highest ideas.

JANE ADDAMS

 **17** Saint Patrick it was
Who started the style —
Let's all wear a bit of green!
For the Irish a cheer,
For the shamrock a smile —
Let's all wear a bit of green!

GRACE L. SCHAUFFLER

 **18** There are two kinds of success. One is the very rare kind that comes to the man who has the power to do what no one else has the power to do. That is genius. But the average man who wins what we call success is not a genius. He is a man who has merely the ordinary qualities that he shares with his fellows, but who has developed those ordinary qualities to a more than ordinary degree.

THEODORE ROOSEVELT

 **19** O beautiful human life! Tears come to my eyes as I think of it. So beautiful, so inexpressibly beautiful! The song should never be silent, the dance never still, the laugh should sound like water which runs forever.

RICHARD JEFFRIES

 **20** Self-respect cannot be hunted. It cannot be pur-
chased. It is never for sale. It cannot be fabricated
out of public relations. It comes to us when we are
alone, in quiet moments, in quiet places, when we
suddenly realize that, knowing the good, we have
done it; knowing the beautiful, we have served it;
knowing the truth, we have spoken it.

WHITNEY GRISWOLD

 **21** Sense is our helmet, wit is but the plume;
The plume exposes, 'tis our helmet saves.
Sense is the diamond, weighty, solid, sound;
When cut by wit, it casts a brighter beam;
Yet, wit apart, it is a diamond still.

EDWARD YOUNG

 **22** I believe that life is given us so we may grow
in love, and I believe that God is in me as the sun
is in the colour and fragrance of a flower —
the Light in my darkness, the Voice in my silence.

HELEN KELLER

 **23** Gratitude is one of those things that cannot be
bought. It must be born with men, or else all the
obligations in the world will not create it. A real
sense of a kind thing is a gift of nature, and
never was, nor can be acquired.

LORD HALIFAX

 **24** Nature has presented us with a large faculty of entertaining ourselves alone; and often calls us to it, to teach us that we owe ourselves partly to society, but chiefly and mostly to ourselves.

MICHEL DE MONTAIGNE

 **25** 'Tis a lesson you should heed,
　　Try, try again;
If at first you don't succeed,
　　Try, try again;
Then your courage should appear,
For, if you will persevere,
You will conquer, never fear;
　　Try, try again.

AUTHOR UNKNOWN

 **26** I still remain convinced that truth, love, peaceableness, meekness, and kindness are the violence which can master all other violence. The world will be theirs as soon as ever a sufficient number of men with purity of heart, with strength, and with perseverance think and live out the thoughts of love and truth, of meekness and peaceableness.

ALBERT SCHWEITZER

 **27** God answers sharp and sudden on some prayers,
And thrusts the thing we have prayed for in our face,
A gauntlet with a gift in 't. — Every wish
Is like a prayer, with God.

ELIZABETH BARRETT BROWNING

 **28** Time is a flowing river. Happy those who allow themselves to be carried, unresisting, with the current. They float through easy days. They live, unquestioning, in the moment.

CHRISTOPHER MORLEY

 **29**

There is much that's good and pure
that will as long as ill endure —
and blessed are they who see it.

W. L. SHOEMAKER

 **30** The will is free;
Strong is the Soul, and wise, and beautiful;
The seeds of godlike power are in us still:
Gods are we, Bards, Saints, Heroes, if we will.

MATTHEW ARNOLD

 **31**

Build a little fence of trust
    Around to-day;
Fill the space with loving work,
    And therein stay;
Look not through the sheltering bars
    Upon to-morrow;
God will help thee bear what comes
    Of joy or sorrow.

MARY FRANCES BUTTS

1

One's philosophy is not best expressed in words;
it is expressed in the choices one makes . . . In the
long run, we shape our lives and we shape ourselves.
The process never ends until we die. And the choices
we make are ultimately our responsibility.

ELEANOR ROOSEVELT

 2

The roofs are shining from the rain,
　　The sparrows twitter as they fly,
And with a windy April grace
　　The little clouds go by.

Yet the back-yards are bare and brown
　　With only one unchanging tree —
I could not be so sure of Spring
　　Save that it sings in me.

SARA TEASDALE

 3

That we should do unto others as we would have
them do unto us — that we should respect the rights
of others as scrupulously as we would have our
rights respected — is not a mere counsel of perfection
to individuals — but it is the law to which we must
conform social institutions and national policy, if we
would secure the blessings and abundance of peace.

HENRY GEORGE

 4

It is only a man's own fundamental thoughts that
have truth and life in them. For it is these that
he really and completely understands. To read the
thoughts of others is like taking the remains of
someone else's meal, like putting on the discarded
clothes of a stranger.

ARTHUR SCHOPENHAUER

5 You wake up in the morning, and lo! your purse is magically filled with twenty-four hours of the unmanufactured tissue of the universe of your life. It is yours. It is the most precious of possessions. No one can take it from you. It is unstealable. And no one receives either more or less than you receive.

ARNOLD BENNETT

 6 No one has success until he has the abounding life. This is made up of the many-fold activity of energy, enthusiasm and gladness. It is to spring to meet the day with a thrill at being alive. It is to go forth to meet the morning in an ecstasy of joy. It is to realize the oneness of humanity in true spiritual sympathy.

LILLIAN WHITING

 7 Be sure to keep a mirror always nigh
In some convenient, handy sort of place,
And now and then look squarely in thine eye,
And with thyself keep ever face to face.

JOHN K. BANGS

 8 I have told you of the man who always put on spectacles when about to eat cherries, in order that the fruit might look larger and more tempting. In like manner I always make the most of my en-joyments, and, though I do not cast my eyes away from troubles, I pack them into as small a compass as I can for myself, and never let them annoy others.

ROBERT SOUTHEY

9

In the creative state a man is taken out of himself.
He lets down as it were a bucket into his subconscious,
and draws up something which is normally beyond
his reach. He mixes this thing with his normal
experiences, and out of the mixture he makes
a work of art.

E.M.FORSTER

 **10**

Conviction brings a silent, indefinable beauty
into faces made of the commonest human clay; the
devout worshipper at any shrine reflects something
of its golden glow, even as the glory of a noble
love shines like a sort of light from
a woman's face.

HONORE DE BALZAC

 **11**

One ship drives east and another west, with the
self-same winds that blow; 'tis the set of the sails
and not the gales that determines where they go.
Like the winds of the sea are the ways of fate, as
we voyage along through life; 'tis the set of a
soul that decides its goal — and not the calm
or the strife.

ELLA WHEELER WILCOX

 **12**

The men whom I have seen succeed best in life
have always been cheerful and hopeful men, who
went about their business with a smile on their faces,
and took the changes and chances of this mortal
life like men, facing rough and smooth alike
as it came.

CHARLES KINGSLEY

 **13** Mystery creates wonder and wonder is the basis for man's desire to understand. Who knows what mysteries will be solved in our lifetime, and what new riddles will become the challenge of the new generations?

NEIL A. ARMSTRONG

 **14** If you persuade yourself that you can do a certain thing, provided this thing be possible, you will do it, however difficult it may be. If, on the contrary, you imagine that you cannot do the simplest thing in the world, it is impossible for you to do it, and molehills become for you unscalable mountains.

ÉMILE COUÉ

 **15** Taxes are indeed very heavy; but if those laid on by the government were the only ones we had to pay, we might more easily discharge them; but we have many others, and much more grievous ones to some of us. We are taxed quite as heavily by idleness, three times as much by our pride, and four times as much by our folly; and from these taxes the commissioners cannot easily deliver us by allowing an abatement.

BENJAMIN FRANKLIN

 **16** Say well is good, but do well is better;
Do well seems the spirit, say well the letter;
Say well is godly and helps to please,
But do well is godly and gives the world ease.

AUTHOR UNKNOWN

 **17**

Love is a mutual confidence whose foundations no one knows. The one I love surpasses all the laws of nature in sureness. Love is capable of any wisdom.

HENRY DAVID THOREAU

 **18**

Is it wholly fantastic to admit the possibility that Nature herself strove toward what we call beauty? Face to face with any one of the elaborate flowers which man's cultivation has had nothing to do with, it does not seem fantastic to me. We put survival first. But when we have a margin of safety left over, we expend it in the search for the beautiful. Who can say that Nature does not do the same?

JOSEPH WOOD KRUTCH

 **19**

The law should be loved a little because it is felt to be just; feared a little because it is severe; hated a little because it is to a certain degree out of sympathy with the prevalent temper of the day; and respected because it is felt to be a necessity.

EMILE FOURGET

 **20**

What a strange power the perception of beauty is! It seems to ebb and flow like some secret tide, independent alike of health or disease, of joy or sorrow. There are times in our lives when we seem to go singing on our way, and when the beauty of the world sets itself like a quiet harmony to the song we uplift.

A.C. BENSON

 **21**

The soul is a fire that darts its rays through all the senses; it is in this fire that existence consists; all the observations and all the efforts of philosophers ought to turn toward this me, the center and moving power of our sentiments and our ideas.

MADAME DE STAEL

 **22**

It is an old maxim of mine that when you have excluded the impossible, whatever remains, however improbable, must be the truth.

SIR ARTHUR CONAN DOYLE

 **23**

In those vernal seasons of the year, when the air is calm and pleasant, it were an injury and sullenness against Nature not to go out, and see her riches, and partake in her rejoicing with heaven and earth.

JOHN MILTON

 **24**

Loveliest of trees, the cherry now
Is hung with bloom along the bough,
And stands about the woodland ride
Wearing white for Eastertide.

A. E. HOUSMAN

 **25**

When you get into a tight place and everything goes against you, till it seems as though you could not hold on a minute longer, never give up then, for that is just the place and the time that the tide will turn.

HARRIET BEECHER STOWE

26 The world judges you by what you have done, not by what you have started out to do; by what you have completed, not by what you have begun. The bulldog wins by the simple expedient of holding on to the finish.

BALTASAR GRACIÁN

27 Is it so small a thing
To have enjoyed the sun,
To have lived light in the spring,
To have loved, to have thought, to have done . . .

MATTHEW ARNOLD

28 I am certain of nothing but the holiness of the heart's affections and the truth of imagination — what the imagination seizes as beauty must be truth — whether it existed before or not.

JOHN KEATS

29 Laughter is the sensation of feeling good all over and showing it principally in one place.

JOSH BILLINGS

30 Wisdom is not finally tested by the schools,
Wisdom cannot be pass'd from one having it to
    another not having it,
Wisdom is of the soul, is not susceptible of proof,
    is its own proof.

WALT WHITMAN

1 Now the bright morning star, day's harbinger,
Comes dancing from the East, and leads with her
The flowry May, who from her green lap throws
The yellow Cowslip and the pale Primrose.

JOHN MILTON

 2 I'm glad the sky is painted blue;
And the earth is painted green;
And such a lot of nice fresh air
All sandwiched in between!

AUTHOR UNKNOWN

 3 Times change, and men's minds with them. Down
the past, civilizations have exposited themselves
in terms of power, of world-power or of other-world
power. No civilization has yet exposited itself
in terms of love-of-man.

JACK LONDON

 4 Tomorrow is the most important thing in life.
Comes into us at midnight very clean. It's perfect
when it arrives and it puts itself in our hands.
It hopes we've learned something from yesterday.

JOHN WAYNE

 5 Never be entirely idle: but either be reading, or
writing, or praying, or meditating, or endeavouring
something for the public good.

THOMAS À KEMPIS

6
Humans are not helpless. They have never been helpless. They have only been deflected or deceived or dispirited. This is not to say their history has not been pockmarked by failure. But failure is not the ultimate fact of life; it is an aspect of life in which transient or poor judgments play larger roles than they should.

NORMAN COUSINS

 7
I live for those who love me, for those who
     know me true;
For the heaven that smiles above me, and awaits
     my spirit too.
For the cause that lacks assistance, for the wrong
     that needs resistance,
For the future in the distance, and the good
     that I can do.

G.L.BANKS

 8
Some say that the age of chivalry is past, that the spirit of romance is dead. The age of chivalry is never past, so long as there is a wrong left unredressed on earth.

CHARLES KINGSLEY

 9
We are like people on a moving sidewalk which is going the wrong way. If we stand still, our goal recedes. If we walk at an easy pace we barely keep from slipping back. Only through extra effort can we win real gains.

HARRY K. WOLFE

 **10**

There is no past we can bring back by longing for it.
There is only an eternally now that builds and
creates out of the past something new and better.

JOHANN WOLFGANG VON GOETHE

 **11**

Experience is never limited, and it is never
complete; it is an immense sensibility, a kind
of huge spider-web of the finest silken threads
suspended in the chamber of consciousness, and
catching every air-borne particle in its tissue.

HENRY JAMES

 **12**

Two things fill the mind with ever-increasing
wonder and awe, the more often and the more
intensely the mind of thought is drawn to them:
the starry heavens above me and the moral law
within me.

IMMANUEL KANT

 **13**

When God thought of mother, He must have
laughed with satisfaction, and framed it quickly —
so rich, so deep, so divine, so full of soul, power
and beauty was the conception.

HENRY WARD BEECHER

 **14**

The clear sky,
The green fruitful earth is good;
But peace among men is better.

OMAHA INDIAN SONG

15 Every successful business in the world is in existence because its founder recognized in a problem or need an opportunity to be of service to others. Every problem or need in your life is in reality an opportunity to call forth inner resources of wisdom, love, strength and ability.

J. SIG PAULSON

16 Once more we are entering a period in which men will have to give their whole attention to what they are doing and in which the safety of the whole group will depend on men and women who, as boys and girls, learned that life in the twentieth century is like a parachute jump; you have to get it right the first time.

MARGARET MEAD

17 Most people do not half realize how sacred a thing a legitimate ambition is. What is this eternal urge within us which is trying to push us on and on, up and up? It is the urge, the push in the great force within us, which is perpetually prodding us to do our best and refuses to accept our second best.

ORISON SWETT MARDEN

18 The main thing is to be honest with yourself, know and recognize your limits and attain maximum achievement within them. I would for example get more satisfaction from climbing Snowdon, which I know I could, than from attempting Everest, which I couldn't.

STIRLING MOSS

 **19** Fishing is the chance to wash one's soul with pure air. It brings meekness and inspiration, reduces our egotism, soothes our troubles and shames our wickedness. It is discipline in the equality of men — for all men are equal before fish.

HERBERT HOOVER

 **20** (Some people) have a wonderful capacity to appreciate again and again, freshly and naively, the basic goods of life, with awe, pleasure, wonder, and even ecstasy.

A. H. MASLOW

 21 Twixt optimist and pessimist,
The difference is droll;
The optimist sees the doughnut,
The pessimist sees the hole.

McLANDBURGH WILSON

 **22** The character and qualifications of the leader are reflected in the men he selects, develops and gathers around him. Show me the leader and I will know his men. Show me the men and I will know their leader.

ARTHUR W. NEWCOMB

 **23** It is common to overlook what is near by keeping the eye fixed on something remote. In the same manner present opportunities are neglected, and attainable good is slighted by minds busied in extensive ranges and intent upon future advantages.

SAMUEL JOHNSON

24 He who helps a child helps humanity with an immediateness which no other help given to human creature in any other stage of human life can possibly give again.

PHILLIPS BROOKS

25 Far away there in the sunshine are my highest aspirations. I may not reach them, but I can look up and see their beauty, believe in them, and try to follow where they lead.

LOUISA MAY ALCOTT

26 To a lady who, looking at an engraving of a house, called it an ugly thing, he said, 'No, madam, there is nothing ugly; I never saw an ugly thing in my life: for let the form of an object be what it may — light, shade, and perspective will always make it beautiful.'

JOHN CONSTABLE

27 In every heart some seed of goodness grows;
　In every path some bud of beauty springs;
In every sky some rainbow color glows;
　In every hedge some woodland warbler sings.

M. A. B. KELLY

28 Climb the mountains and get their good tidings. Nature's peace will flow into you as sunshine flows into trees. The winds will blow their own freshness into you, and the storms their energy, while cares will drop away from you like the leaves of Autumn.

JOHN MUIR

29

There is a tide in the affairs of men
Which taken at the flood leads on to fortune;
Omitted, all the voyage of their life
Is bound in shallows and in miseries.
On such a full sea are we now afloat,
And we must take the current when it serves,
Or lose our ventures.

WILLIAM SHAKESPEARE

30

How shall we honor them, our Deathless Dead?
How keep their mighty memories alive?
In him who feels their passion, they survive!
Flatter their souls with deeds, and all is said!

EDWIN MARKHAM

31

To me it seems that when God
conceived the world,
that was poetry;
He formed it,
and that was sculpture;
He varied and colored it,
and that was painting;
and then, crowned all,
He peopled it with living beings,
and that was the grand, divine,
eternal drama.

CHARLOTTE CUSHMAN

JUNE

 1

Do not be afraid of showing your affection.
Be warm and tender, thoughtful and affectionate.
Men are more helped by sympathy, than by service;
love is more than money, and a kind word will
give more pleasure than a present.

JOHN LUBBOCK

 2

It is easy in the world to live after the world's
opinion; it is easy in solitude to live after our own;
but the great man is he who in the midst of the crowd
keeps with perfect sweetness the independence
of his solitude.

RALPH WALDO EMERSON

 3

Well, look at an animal, a cat, a dog, or a bird,
or one of those beautiful great beasts in the zoo,
a puma or a giraffe. You can't help seeing that all
of them are right. They're never in any embarrass-
ment. They always know what to do and how to
behave themselves. They don't flatter and they
don't intrude. They don't pretend. They are as
they are, like stones or flowers or stars in the sky.
Don't you agree?

HERMANN HESSE

 4

We are made for cooperation, like feet, like hands,
like eyelids, like the rows of the upper and lower
teeth. To act against one another is contrary to
nature, and it is acting against one another to be
vexed and to turn away.

MARCUS AURELIUS

5

When I was a boy of fourteen, my father was so ignorant I could hardly stand to have the old man around. But when I got to be twenty-one I was astonished at how much the old man had learned in seven years.

MARK TWAIN

 6

The first of our senses which we should take care never to let rust through disuse is that sixth sense, the imagination. I mean the wide open eye which leads us always to see truth more vividly, to apprehend more broadly, to concern ourselves more deeply, to be, all our life long, sensitive and awake to the powers and responsibilities given to us as human beings.

CHRISTOPHER FRY

 7

The Camel's hump is an ugly lump
Which well you may see at the Zoo;
But uglier yet is the Hump we get
From having too little to do.

RUDYARD KIPLING

 8

Sometimes looking deep into the eyes of a child, you are conscious of meeting a glance full of wisdom. The child has known nothing yet but love and beauty. All this piled-up world knowledge you have acquired is unguessed at by him. And yet you meet this wonderful look that tells you in a moment more than all the years of experience have seemed to teach.

HILDEGARDE HAWTHORNE

9 I would like to have engraved inside every wedding band, *Be kind to one another.* This is the Golden Rule of marriage, and the secret of making love last through the years.

RANDOLPH RAY

 **10** I have never been bored an hour in my life. I get up every morning wondering what new strange glamorous thing is going to happen and it happens at fairly regular intervals. Lady Luck has been good to me and I fancy she has been good to every one. Only some people are dour, and when she gives them the come hither with her eyes, they look down or turn away and lift an eyebrow. But me, I give her the wink and away we go.

WILLIAM ALLEN WHITE

 **11** There is no friend like an old friend
Who has shared our morning days,
No greeting like his welcome,
No homage like his praise.

OLIVER WENDELL HOLMES

 **12** We merely want to live in peace with all the world, to trade with them, to commune with them, to learn from their culture as they may learn from ours . . . so that the products of our toil may be used for our schools and our roads and our churches and not for guns and planes and tanks and ships of war.

DWIGHT D. EISENHOWER

 **13**

I think that the ideals of youth are fine, clear
and unencumbered; and that the real art of living
consists in keeping alive the conscience and sense
of values we had when we were young.

ROCKWELL KENT

 14

Hear the mellow wedding bells —
   Golden bells!
What a world of happiness their harmony
   foretells!

EDGAR ALLAN POE

 **15**

I live on the sunny side of the street; shady folks
live on the other. I have always preferred the
sunshine and have tried to put other people there,
if only for an hour or two at a time.

MARSHALL P. WILDER

 **16**

Order means light and peace, inward liberty and
free command over oneself; order is power.

HENRI-FRÉDÉRIC AMIEL

 **17**

Leadership is complicated. It is intellectual;
it is emotional; and it is physical. It is inherited,
and it is learned. It is the summation of the total
man which must square with the myriad desires
of the group.

EMERY STOOPS

 **18** Those who decide to use leisure as a means of mental development, who love good music, good books, good pictures, good plays, good company, good conversation — what are they? They are the happiest people in the world.

WILLIAM LYON PHELPS

 **19** What is a plan? A plan is a method of action, procedure, or arrangement. It is a program to be done. It is a design to carry into effect, an idea, a thought, a project, or a development. Therefore, a plan is a concrete means to help you fulfill your desires.

EARL PREVETTE

 **20**
When a bit of sunshine hits ye,
  After passing of a cloud,
When a fit of laughter gits ye
  And ye'r spine is feelin' proud,
Don't forget to up and fling it
  At a soul that's feelin' blue,
For the minit that ye sling it
  It's a boomerang to you.

CAPT. JACK CRAWFORD

 **21** Summer is a sailor in a rowboat and ice-cream on your dress when you're four years old. Summer is a man with his coat off, wet sand between your toes, the smell of a garden an hour before moonrise. Oh, summer is silk itself, a giant geranium and music from a flute far away!

MICHAEL BROWN

 **22** The beauty that addresses itself to the eyes is only the spell of the moment; the eye of the body is not always that of the soul.

GEORGE SAND

 **23** Most arts require long study and application; but the most useful of all, that of pleasing, only the desire.

LORD CHESTERFIELD

 **24** Progress, man's distinctive mark alone,
Not God's, and not the beasts';
God is, they are;
Man partly is, and wholly hopes to be.

ROBERT BROWNING

 **25** Each time a man stands up for an ideal, or acts to improve the lot of others, or strikes out against injustice, he sends forth a tiny ripple of hope . . . and crossing each other from a million different centers of energy and daring those ripples build a current that can sweep down the mightiest walls of oppression and resistance.

ROBERT F. KENNEDY

 **26** Why thus longing, thus forever sighing
For the far-off, unattain'd, and dim
While the beautiful all round thee lying
Offers up its low, perpetual hymn?

HARRIET W. SEWALL

 **27**

The refuge from pessimism is the good men and women at any time existing in the world, — they keep faith and happiness alive.

CHARLES E. NORTON

 **28**

Whatever you are by nature, keep to it; never desert your own line of talent. Be what nature intended you for, and you will succeed; be anything else and you will be ten thousand times worse than nothing.

SYDNEY SMITH

 **29**

Reputation said: "If once we sever,
Our chance of future meeting is but vain;
Who parts from me, must look to part for ever,
For Reputation lost comes not again."

CHARLES LAMB

 **30**

Many a genius has been slow of growth. Oaks that flourish for a thousand years do not spring up into beauty like a reed.

GEORGE HENRY LEWES

1
It is a glorious privilege to live, to know, to act,
to listen, to behold, to love. To look up at the blue
summer sky; to see the sun sink slowly beyond
the line of the horizon; to watch the worlds come
twinkling into view, first one by one, and the
myriads that no man can count, and lo!
the universe is white with them; and you
and I are here.

MARCO MORROW

 2
I would define liberty to be a power to do as we
would be done by. The definition of liberty to be
the power of doing whatever the law permits,
meaning the civil laws, does not seem
satisfactory.

JOHN ADAMS

 3
Freedom is an indivisible word. If we want to
enjoy it, and fight for it, we must be prepared to
extend it to everyone, whether they are rich or poor,
whether they agree with us or not, no matter what
their race or the color of their skin.

WENDELL WILLKIE

 4
We take the stars from heaven, the red from our
mother country, separating it by white stripes,
thus showing that we have separated from her,
and the white stripes shall go down to posterity,
representing our liberty.

GEORGE WASHINGTON

5 We live in deeds, not years; in thoughts, not breaths;
In feelings, not in figures on a dial.
We should count time by heart-throbs.
      He most lives
Who thinks most, feels the noblest, acts the best.

PHILIP JAMES BAILEY

 6 Evening after evening in the summer, I have gone
to see the white clover fall asleep in the meadow.
   Kneeling and looking very closely, one sees the
two lower leaves on each stalk gently approach one
another like little hands that were going to clap
but thought better of it, and at last lie folded
quietly as though for prayer.
   Then the upper leaf droops, as a child's face
might, until it rests on the others.
   Everywhere in the dusk the white clover leaves
are sleeping in an attitude of worship.

MARY WEBB

 7 The earth hums to me to-day in the sun, like a woman
at her spinning, some ballad of the ancient time
in a forgotten tongue.

RABINDRANATH TAGORE

 8 There is nothing holier in this life of ours than
the first consciousness of love — the first fluttering
of its silken wings — the first rising sound and
breath of that wind which is so soon to sweep
through the soul, to purify or to destroy.

HENRY WADSWORTH LONGFELLOW

9

One of the most important, but one of the most difficult things for a powerful mind is, to be its own master. A pond may lie quiet in a plain; but a lake wants mountains to compass and hold it in.

JOSEPH ADDISON

 **10**

And truly, I reiterate, nothing's small!
No lily-muffled hum of a summer bee,
But finds some coupling with the spinning stars;
No pebble at your foot, but proves a sphere;
No chaffinch, but implies the cherubim.

ELIZABETH BARRETT BROWNING

 **11**

Workers earn it,   Heirs receive it,
Spendthrifts burn it,   Thrifty save it,
Bankers lend it,   Misers crave it,
Women spend it,   Robbers seize it,
Forgers fake it,   Rich increase it,
Taxes take it,   Gamblers lose it . . .
Dying leave it,   I could use it.

RICHARD ARMOUR

 **12**

As rivers have their source in some far off fountain, so the human spirit has its source. To find his fountain of spirit is to learn the secret of heaven and earth.

LAO TZU

 **13**

If you have great talents, industry will improve them: if you have but moderate abilities, industry will supply their deficiency.

SIR JOSHUA REYNOLDS

 **14** Certain thoughts are prayers. There are moments when, whatever be the attitude of the body, the soul is on its knees.

VICTOR HUGO

 **15** Every human being has some handle by which he may be lifted, some groove in which he was meant to run; and the great work of his life, as far as our relations with each other are concerned, is to lift each one by his own proper handle, and run each one in his own proper groove.

HARRIET BEECHER STOWE

 **16** The wise bustle and laugh as they walk in the pageant, but fools bustle and are important; and this probably is all the difference between them.

OLIVER GOLDSMITH

 **17** Three passions, simple but overwhelmingly strong, have governed my life: the longing for love, the search for knowledge, and unbearable pity for the suffering of mankind.

BERTRAND RUSSELL

 **18** I studied the lives of great men and famous women, and I found that the men and women who got to the top were those who did the jobs they had in hand, with everything they had of energy and enthusiasm and hard work.

HARRY S. TRUMAN

 **19** Our great thoughts, our great affections, the truths of our life, never leave us. Surely they cannot separate from our consciousness, shall follow it withersoever that shall go, and are of their nature divine and immortal.

WILLIAM MAKEPEACE THACKERAY

 **20** When a man sits with a pretty girl for an hour, it seems like a minute. But let him sit on a hot stove for a minute — and it's longer than any hour. That's relativity.

ALBERT EINSTEIN

 **21** How pleasant it is, at the end of the day,
No follies to have to repent;
But reflect on the past, and be able to say,
That my time has been properly spent.

JANE TAYLOR

 **22** Affection can withstand very severe storms of vigor, but not a long polar frost of indifference.

SIR WALTER SCOTT

 **23** Integrity is the first step to true greatness. —
Men love to praise, but are slow to practice it. —
To maintain it in high places costs self-denial;
in all places it is liable to opposition, but its
end is glorious, and the universe will yet
do it homage.

CHARLES SIMMONS

 **24** Nature, like a loving mother, is ever trying to keep land and sea, mountain and valley, each in its place, to hush the angry winds and waves, balance the extremes of heat and cold, of rain and drought, that peace, harmony and beauty may reign supreme.

ELIZABETH CADY STANTON

 **25** Men are tattooed with their special beliefs like so many South Sea Islanders; but a real human heart with divine love in it beats with the same glow under all the patterns of all earth's thousand tribes.

OLIVER WENDELL HOLMES

 **26** The earth's distances invite the eye. And as the eye reaches, so must the mind stretch to meet these new horizons. I challenge anyone to stand with autumn on a hilltop and fail to see a new expanse not only around him, but in him, too.

HAL BORLAND

 **27** Man is incomprehensible without Nature, and Nature is incomprehensible apart from man. For the delicate loveliness of the flower is as much in the human eye as in its own fragile petals, and the splendor of the heavens as much in the imagination that kindles at the touch of their glory as in the shining of countless worlds.

HAMILTON WRIGHT MABIE

 **28** Remember that the most beautiful things in the world are the most useless; peacocks and lilies, for instance.

JOHN RUSKIN

 **29** Lord, make me an instrument of Thy peace;
Where hate rules, let me bring love;
Where malice, forgiveness;
Where disputes, reconciliation;
Where error, truth;
Where despair, hope;
Where darkness, Thy light;
Where sorrow, joy.

ST. FRANCIS OF ASSISI

 **30** I have learned that success is to be measured not so much by the position that one has reached in life as by the obstacles which he has overcome while trying to succeed.

BOOKER T. WASHINGTON

 **31** Awake my soul, and with the sun
Thy daily stage of duty run;
Shake off dull sloth, and joyful rise
To pay thy morning sacrifice.

BISHOP THOMAS KEN

AUGUST

 1

It is probably a pity that every citizen of each state cannot visit all the others, to see the differences, to learn what we have in common, and to come back with a richer, fuller understanding of America — in all its beauty, in all its dignity, in all its strength, in support of moral principle.

DWIGHT D. EISENHOWER

 2

He is an eloquent man who can treat humble subjects with delicacy, lofty things impressively and moderate things temperately.

CICERO

 3

Our creator would never have made such lovely days, and have given us the deep hearts to enjoy them, above and beyond all thought, unless we were meant to be immortal.

NATHANIEL HAWTHORNE

 4

You must learn day by day, year by year, to broaden your horizon. The more things you love, the more you are interested in, the more you enjoy, the more you are indignant about — the more you have left when anything happens.

ETHEL BARRYMORE

 5

Culture, the acquainting ourselves with the best that has been known and said in the world, and thus with the history of the human spirit.

MATTHEW ARNOLD

6 Love is much nicer to be in than an automobile accident, a tight girdle, a higher tax bracket or a holding pattern over Philadelphia.

JUDITH VIORST

 7 Who of us is mature enough for offspring before the offspring themselves arrive? The value of marriage is not that adults produce children but that children produce adults.

PETER DE VRIES

 8 The song is to the singer, and comes back
most to him,
The teaching is to the teacher, and comes back
most to him,
The love is to the lover, and comes back
most to him.

WALT WHITMAN

 9 The best cure for worry, depression, melancholy, brooding, is to go deliberately forth and try to lift with one's sympathy the gloom of somebody else.

ARNOLD BENNETT

 **10** It is an interesting question how far men would retain their relative rank if they were divested of their clothes. Could you in such a case tell surely of any company of civilized men which belong to the respected class?

HENRY DAVID THOREAU

11 The happiness of life is made up of minute fractions — the little soon forgotten charities of a kiss or smile, a kind look, a heartfelt compliment, and the countless infinitesimals of pleasurable and genial feeling.

SAMUEL TAYLOR COLERIDGE

12 It is better to have loafed and lost then never to have loafed at all.

JAMES THURBER

13 Shut your eyes and you will know what I mean by thought entombed in darkness. Light comes through the senses, and not only through the sense of sight. When you see without feeling, you are still partly blind; you lack the inner light that brings awareness. Awareness requires the interplay of every faculty, the use of your entire being as an eye.

CHARLES A. LINDBERGH

14 Destiny is not a matter of chance, it is a matter of choice; it is not a thing to be waited for, it is a thing to be achieved.

WILLIAM JENNINGS BRYAN

15 Ringling Brothers Circus has been called the greatest show on earth, but I think when the history of our times has been written, they will say that an American political convention is the greatest show on earth.

BILLY GRAHAM

 **16** Anything will give up its secrets if you love it
enough. Not only have I found that when I talk to
the little flower or to the little peanut they will
give up their secrets, but I have found that when
I silently commune with people they give up their
secrets also — if you love them enough.

GEORGE WASHINGTON CARVER

17 Man is his own star; and the soul that can
Render an honest and perfect man
Commands all light, all influence, all fate;
Nothing to him falls early or too late.

BEAUMONT AND FLETCHER

18 Any piece of knowledge I acquire today has a value
at this moment exactly proportioned to my skill to
deal with it. Tomorrow, when I know more, I recall
that piece of knowledge and use it better.

MARK VAN DOREN

19 The sincerest satisfactions in life come in doing
and not in dodging duty; in meeting and solving
problems, in facing facts, in being a dependable
person.

RICHARD L. EVANS

20 The real difference between men is energy. A strong
will, a settled purpose, an invincible determination,
can accomplish almost anything; and in this lies the
distinction between great men and little men.

THOMAS FULLER

21 Courtesy is a science of the highest importance. It is like grace and beauty in the body, which charm at first sight, and lead on to further intimacy and friendship.

MICHEL DE MONTAIGNE

22 We must have courage to bet on our ideas, to take the calculated risk, and to act. Everyday living requires courage if life is to be effective and bring happiness.

MAXWELL MALTZ

23 Art creates an atmosphere in which the proprieties, the amenities, and the virtues unconsciously grow. The rain does not lecture the seed. The light does not make rules for the vine and flower. The heart is softened by the pathos of the perfect.

ROBERT G. INGERSOLL

24 The true foundation of the brotherhood of man is belief in the knowledge that God is the Father of mankind. For us, therefore, brotherhood is not only a generous impulse but also a divine command.

HARRY S. TRUMAN

25 I think it rather fine, this necessity for the tense bracing of the will before anything worth doing can be done. I rather like it myself. I feel it is to be the chief thing that differentiates me from the cat by the fire.

ARNOLD BENNETT

 **26**

The quality of mercy is not strain'd,
It droppeth as the gentle rain from heaven
Upon the place beneath: it is twice blest;
It blesseth him that gives, and him that takes.

WILLIAM SHAKESPEARE

 **27**

The real joy of life is in its play. Play is anything
we do for the joy and love of doing it, apart from
any profit, compulsion, or sense of duty.
It is the real living of life with the feeling of
freedom and self-expression. Play is the business
of childhood, and its continuation in later years
is the prolongation of youth.

WALTER RAUSCHENBUSCH

 **28**

The tree which moves some to tears of joy is in the
eyes of others only a green thing which stands in the
way. To the eyes of the man of imagination Nature
is Imagination itself. As a man is, so he sees.

WILLIAM BLAKE

 **29**

Grow old along with me!
The best is yet to be,
The last of life, for which the first was made:
Our times are in his hand
Who saith, "A whole I planned,
Youth shows but half; trust God: see all,
    nor be afraid!"

ROBERT BROWNING

AUGUST

 **30** The longer I live the more my mind dwells upon the beauty and the wonder of the world. I hardly know which feeling leads, wonderment or admiration.

JOHN BURROUGHS

 **31** All things bright and beautiful,
All creatures great and small,
All things wise and wonderful,
The Lord God made them all.

CECIL FRANCES ALEXANDER

SEPTEMBER

 1 God made sun and moon to distinguish the seasons, and day and night; and we cannot have the fruits of the earth but in their seasons. But God hath made no decrees to distinguish the seasons of His mercies. In Paradise the fruits were ripe the first minute, and in Heaven it is always autumn. His mercies are ever in their maturity.

JOHN DONNE

 2 There is too little idea of personal responsibility; too much of "the world owes me a living," forgetting that if the world does owe you a living you yourself must be your own collector.

THEODORE N. VAIL

3

There is no real wealth but the labor of man.
Were the mountains of gold and the valleys of silver,
the world would not be one grain of corn the richer;
no one comfort would be added to the human race.

PERCY BYSSHE SHELLEY

 4

All things are literally better, lovelier,
and more beloved for the imperfections which have
been divinely appointed, that the law of human
life may be Effort, and the law of
human judgment, Mercy.

JOHN RUSKIN

 5

Love your children with all your hearts, love them
enough to discipline them before it is too late . . .
Praise them for important things, even if you have
to stretch them a bit. Praise them a lot. They live
on it like bread and butter and they need it more
than bread and butter.

LAVINA CHRISTENSEN FUGAL

 6

School days, school days, dear old
    golden rule days;
Readin' and 'ritin' and 'rithmetic,
Taught to the tune of a hick'ry stick,
You were my queen in calico,
I was your bashful, barefoot beau,
And you wrote on my slate,
"I love you, Joe,"
When we were a couple of kids.

WILL D. COBB

SEPTEMBER

 7
Civilization is the encouragement of differences. Civilization thus becomes a synonym of democracy. Force, violence, pressure, or compulsion with a view to conformity, is both uncivilized and undemocratic.

MOHANDAS GANDHI

 8
Season of mists and mellow fruitfulness,
    Close bosom-friend of the maturing sun;
Conspiring with him how to load and bless
    With fruit the vines that round the
        thatch-eaves run . . .

JOHN KEATS

 9
We should all be concerned about the future because we will have to spend the rest of our lives there.

CHARLES F. KETTERING

 **10**
There is no easy system for formulating questions. Your questions follow the pattern of your thinking. You might remember that the seven interrogative pronouns are who? when? which? what? how? where? and why? They do not cover all the questions you can frame but they can give you a grip on many a problem.

EDWARD HODNETT

 **11**
A handful of pine-seed will cover mountains with the green majesty of forest. I too will set my face to the wind and throw my handful of seed on high.

FIONA MACLEOD

 **12** It is noble to seek truth, and it is beautiful to find it. It is the ancient feeling of the human heart — that knowledge is better than riches; and it is deeply and sacredly true.

SYDNEY SMITH

 **13** We should be careful to get out of an experience only the wisdom that is in it — and stop there; lest we be like the cat that sits down on a hot stove-lid. She will never sit down on a hot stove-lid again — and that is well; but also she will never sit down on a cold one anymore.

MARK TWAIN

 **14**

Have you had a kindness shown?
Pass it on;
'Twas not given for thee alone,
Pass it on;
Let it travel down the years,
Let it wipe another's tears,
Till in Heaven the deed appears —
Pass it on.

HENRY BURTON

 **15** Color, like fragrance, is intimately connected with light; and between the different rays of the spectrum and the color cells of plants there is a strange telepathy. These processes, so little explored, seem in their deep secrecy and earthly spirituality more marvelous than the most radiant visions of the mystics.

MARY WEBB

 **16**

Our dignity consists, then, wholly in thought.
Our elevation must come from this, not from space
and time, which we cannot fill. Let us, then, labor
to think well: that is the fundamental principle
of morals.

BLAISE PASCAL

 **17**

You can not believe in honor until you have achieved
it. Better keep yourself clean and bright; you are
the window through which you must see the world.

GEORGE BERNARD SHAW

 **18**

In short, in life, as in a football game,
the principle to follow is:
Hit the line hard; don't foul and don't shirk;
but hit the line hard!

THEODORE ROOSEVELT

 **19**

Beauty does not lie in the face. It lies in the
harmony between man and his industry. Beauty is
expression. When I paint a mother I try to render her
beautiful by the mere look she gives her child.

JEAN FRANCOIS MILLET

 **20**

The world is a looking-glass, and gives back to
every man the reflection of his own face. Frown at
it, and it in turn will look sourly on you; laugh
at it and with it, and it is a jolly, kind
companion.

WILLIAM MAKEPEACE THACKERAY

 **21**

Give me my scallop shell of quiet,
My staff of faith to walk upon,
My script of joy, immortal diet,
My bottle of salvation,
My gown of glory, hope's true gage,
And thus I'll take my pilgrimage.

SIR WALTER RALEIGH

 **22**

The truth (is) that there is only one terminal dignity
— love. And the story of a love is not important —
what is important is that one is capable of love.
It is perhaps the only glimpse we are permitted
of eternity.

HELEN HAYES

 **23**

The secret of seeing is to sail on solar wind. Hone
and spread your spirit till you yourself are a sail,
whetted, translucent, broadside to the merest puff.

ANNIE DILLARD

 **24**

I cannot praise a fugitive and cloistered virtue,
unexercised and unbreathed, that never sallies out
and sees her adversary, but slinks out of the race,
where the immortal garland is to be run for,
not without dust and heat.

JOHN MILTON

 **25**

Ever insurgent let me be,
Make me more daring than devout;
From sleek contentment keep me free,
And fill me with a buoyant doubt.

LOUIS UNTERMEYER

 **26** The art of conversation is to be prompt without being stubborn, to refute without argument, and to clothe great matters in a motley garb.

BENJAMIN DISRAELI

 **27** The realization that our small planet is only one of many worlds gives mankind the perspective it needs to realize sooner that our own world belongs to all of its creatures, that the moon landing marks the end of our childhood as a race and the beginning of a newer and better civilization.

ARTHUR C. CLARKE

 **28** My creed is this:
Happiness is the only good.
The place to be happy is here.
The time to be happy is now.
The way to be happy is to make others so.

ROBERT G. INGERSOLL

 **29** Luck means the hardships and privations which you have not hesitated to endure; the long nights you have devoted to work. Luck means the appointments you have never failed to keep; the trains you have never failed to catch.

MAX O'RELL

 **30** There are two worlds; the world that we can measure with line and rule, and the world that we feel with our hearts and imagination.

LEIGH HUNT

1

I am in love with this world . . . I have climbed its mountains, roamed its forests, sailed its waters, crossed its deserts, felt the sting of its frosts, the oppression of its heats, the drench of its rains, the fury of its winds, and always have beauty and joy waited upon my goings and comings.

JOHN BURROUGHS

2

Some have narrowed their minds, and so fettered them with the chains of antiquity that not only do they refuse to speak save as the ancients spake, but they refuse to think save as the ancients thought. God speaks to us, too, and the best thoughts are those now being vouchsafed to us. We will excel the ancients!

SAVONAROLA

3

The consciousness of being loved softens the keenest pang, even at the moment of parting; yea, even the eternal farewell is robbed of half its bitterness when uttered in accents that breathe love to the last sigh.

JOSEPH ADDISON

4

When the first light dawned on the earth, and the birds awoke, and the brave river was heard rippling confidently seaward, and the nimble early rising wind rustled the oak leaves about our tent, all men, having reinforced their bodies and their souls with sleep, and cast aside doubt and fear, were invited to unattempted adventures.

HENRY DAVID THOREAU

5
Autumn . . . when the leaves took on the most wonderful golden colors — as if God wanted to adorn them one last time before they fell and died and were swept away by the wind.

LIV ULLMANN

 6
A book is the only place in which you can examine a fragile thought without breaking it, or explore an explosive idea without fear it will go off in your face . . . It is one of the few havens remaining where a man's mind can get both provocation and privacy.

EDWARD P. MORGAN

 7
O suns and skies and flowers of June,
   Count all your boasts together,
Love loveth best of all the year
   October's bright blue weather.

HELEN HUNT JACKSON

 8
Life is beautiful to whomsoever will think beautiful thoughts. There are no common people but they who think commonly and without imagination or beauty. Such are dull enough.

STANTON DAVIS KIRKHAM

 9
It is not he that enters upon any career, or starts in any race, but he that runs well and perseveringly that gains the plaudits of others, or the approval of his own conscience.

ALEXANDER CAMPBELL

10 . . . neither great nor good things were ever attained without loss and hardships. He that would reap and not labour, must faint with the wind, and perish in disappointments; but an hair of my head shall not fall, without the providence of my Father that is over all.

WILLIAM PENN

11
The morns are meeker than they were,
The nuts are getting brown;
The berry's cheek is plumper,
The rose is out of town.

The maple wears a gayer scarf,
The field a scarlet gown.
Lest I should be old-fashioned,
I'll put a trinket on.

EMILY DICKINSON

12
One poor day! —
Remember whose and not how short it is!
It is God's day, it is Columbus's.
A lavish day! One day, with life and heart,
Is more than time enough to find a world.

JAMES RUSSELL LOWELL

13
Flower in the crannied wall,
I pluck you out of the crannies,
I hold you here, root and all, in my hand,
Little flower — but *if* I could understand
What you are, root and all, and all in all,
I should know what God and man is.

ALFRED, LORD TENNYSON

 **14** I expect to pass through the world but once.
Any good therefore that I can do, or any kindness
that I can show to any fellow creature, let me do
it now. Let me not defer or neglect it, for
I shall not pass this way again.

STEPHEN GRELLET

 **15** The secret of happiness is not in doing what one
likes, but in liking what one has to do.

JAMES M. BARRIE

 **16** O grant me, Heaven, a middle state,
Neither too humble nor too great;
More than enough, for nature's ends,
With something left to treat my friends.

DAVID MALLET

 **17** The thought that prompted and was conveyed in a
caress would only lose to be set down in words — ay,
although Shakespeare himself should be the scribe.

ROBERT LOUIS STEVENSON

 **18** From gold to gray
Our mild sweet day
Of Indian summer fades too soon,
But tenderly
Above the sea
Hangs, white and calm, the hunter's moon.

JOHN GREENLEAF WHITTIER

 **19**

It matters not how strait the gate,
　How charged with punishments the scroll,
I am the master of my fate;
　I am the captain of my soul.

WILLIAM ERNEST HENLEY

 **20**

The great secret of success is to go through life
as a man who never gets used up. That is possible
for him who never argues and strives with men and
facts, but in all experience retires upon himself,
and looks for the ultimate cause of things
in himself.

ALBERT SCHWEITZER

 **21**

If our lives shall be such that we shall receive the glad
welcome of "Well done, good and faithful servant,"
we shall then know that we have not lived in vain.

PETER COOPER

 **22**

The manner in which one single ray of light, one
single precious hint, will clarify and energize the
whole mental life of him who receives it, is among
the most wonderful and heavenly of intellectual
phenomena.

ARNOLD BENNETT

 **23**

Be not afraid of greatness: some are born great,
some achieve greatness and some have greatness
thrust upon 'em.

WILLIAM SHAKESPEARE

 **24**

The sublime and the ridiculous are often so nearly related that it is difficult to class them separately. One step above the sublime makes the ridiculous, and one step above the ridiculous makes the sublime again.

THOMAS PAINE

 **25**

Fame is what you have taken,
Character's what you give;
When to this truth you waken,
Then you begin to live.

BAYARD TAYLOR

 **26**

For every beauty there is an eye somewhere to see it.
For every truth there is an ear somewhere to hear it.
For every love there is a heart somewhere to receive it.
But though my beauty meet no eye it still doth glow.
Though my truth meet no ear it still doth shine.
But when my love meets no heart it can only break.

IVAN PANIN

 **27**

When the outlook is steeped in pessimism, I remind myself, "Two and two still make four, and you can't keep mankind down for long."

BERNARD M. BARUCH

 **28**

You can conquer almost any fear if you will only make up your mind to do so. For remember, fear doesn't exist anywhere except in the mind.

DALE CARNEGIE

 **29**

Know all the good that individuals find,
Or God and Nature meant to mere mankind.
Reason's whole pleasure, all the joys of sense,
Lie in these three words — Health, Peace,
and Competence.

ALEXANDER POPE

 **30**

The root of the matter, if we want a stable world,
is a very simple and old-fashioned thing, a thing
so simple that I am almost ashamed to mention it
for fear of the derisive smile with which wise cynics
will greet my words. The thing I mean is love,
Christian love, or compassion. If you feel this, you
have a motive for existence, a reason for courage,
an imperative necessity for intellectual honesty.

BERTRAND RUSSELL

 **31**

A jack-o'-lantern I will make.
I have a pumpkin yellow.
When I get through carving him,
He'll be a jolly fellow.
It's not the time for gloomy looks,
It's not the time of year.
I'll carve a smile upon his face
That goes from ear to ear.

ETTA F. GILBERT

NOVEMBER

 1
When I am working on a problem, I never think about beauty. I think only how to solve the problem. But when I have finished, if the solution is not beautiful, I know it is wrong.

BUCKMINSTER FULLER

 2
Keep coming back, and though the world may romp
    across your spine,
Let every game's end find you still upon
    the battling line:
For when the One Great Scorer comes to mark
    against your name,
He writes — not that you won or lost — but how
    you played the game.

GRANTLAND RICE

 3
Peace! and no longer from its brazen portals
    The blast of War's great organ shakes the skies!
But beautiful as songs of the immortals,
    The holy melodies of love arise.

HENRY WADSWORTH LONGFELLOW

 4
Good words do more than hard speeches, as the sunbeams, without any noise, will make the traveler cast off his cloak, which all the blustering winds could not do, but only make him bind it closer to him.

ROBERT LEIGHTON

 5
Beauty is Nature's coin, must not be hoarded,
But must be current, and the good thereof
Consists in mutual and partaken bliss . . .

JOHN MILTON

6 The foundation of all democracy is that the people have the right to vote. To deprive them of that right is to make a mockery of all the high-sounding phrases which are so often used. At the bottom of all the tributes paid to democracy is the little man, walking into the little booth, with a little pencil, making a little cross on a little bit of paper — no amount of rhetoric or voluminous discussion can possibly diminish the overwhelming importance of that point.

WINSTON CHURCHILL

 7 Sometimes it is said that man cannot be trusted with the government of himself. Can he, then, be trusted with the government of others? Or have we found angels in the forms of kings to govern him? Let history answer this question.

THOMAS JEFFERSON

 8 All higher motives, ideals, conceptions, sentiments in a man are of no account if they do not come forward to strengthen him for the better discharge of the duties which devolve upon him in the ordinary affairs of men.

HENRY WARD BEECHER

 9 Quality is never an accident; it is always the result of high intention, sincere effort, intelligent direction and skillful execution; it represents the wise choice of many alternatives, the cumulative experience of many masters of craftsmanship. Quality also marks the search for an ideal after necessity has been satisfied and mere usefulness achieved.

WILLA A. FOSTER

NOVEMBER

10 Reverence the simple, the prosaic, the natural, the real, but demand of every common thing of life, whether it be your body or your money or your daily experience, that it shall bloom into fine results in your own soul and in your influence upon the world.

PHILLIPS BROOKS

11
Silent is the dark
    Before the sun-beams come,
Yet if it were not for the lark,
    The dawn would be as dumb,

And thus my soul would be
    As dark and still as the night,
If it were not for the minstrelsy
    Of Hope that sings of Light.

FRANCIS CARLIN

12 Few of us, indeed realize the wonderful privilege of living; the blessings we inherit, the glories and beauties of the universe, which is our own if we choose to have it so; the extent to which we can make ourselves what we wish to be; or the power we possess of securing peace, of triumphing over pain and sorrow.

JOHN LUBBOCK

13 Where we cannot invent, we may at least improve; we may give somewhat of novelty to that which was old, condensation to that which was diffuse, perspicuity to that which was obscure, and currency to that which was recondite.

CALEB COLTON

14 These have I loved:
White plates and cups, clean-gleaming,
Ringed with blue lines; and feathery, faery dust;
Wet roofs, beneath the lamp-light; the strong crust
Of friendly bread; and many-tasting food;
Rainbows; and the blue bitter smoke of wood.

RUPERT BROOKE

15 Most people are just like cats in that if you rub
them the right way, they will purr, but if you
rub them the wrong way, they will bite and scratch.

WILLIAM ROSS

16 Isn't it strange
That princes and kings,
And clowns that caper
In sawdust rings,
And common people
Like you and me
Are builders for eternity?

Each is given a bag of tools,
A shapeless mass,
A book of rules;
And each must make —
Ere life has flown —
A stumbling block
Or a steppingstone.

R. L. SHARPE

17 The keen spirit
Seizes the prompt occasion — makes the thought
Start into instant action, and at once
Plans and performs, resolves and executes.

HANNAH MORE

18 Eccentricity has always abounded where strength of character has abounded; and the amount of eccentricity in a society has generally been proportional to the amount of genius, mental vigor, and moral courage which it contained. That so few now dare to be eccentric marks the chief danger of the time.

JOHN STUART MILL

19 Kind words are the music of the world. They have a power that seems to be beyond natural causes, as though they were some angel's song which had lost its way and come back to earth.

FREDERICK WILLIAM FABER

20 An honest reputation is within the reach of all men; they obtain it by social virtues, and by doing their duty. This kind of reputation, it is true, is neither brilliant nor startling, but it is often the most useful for happiness.

CHARLES PINOT DUCLOS

21 I wish you humor and a twinkle in the eye.
I wish you glory and the strength to bear
its burdens.
I wish you sunshine on your path and storms to
season your journey.
I wish you peace — in the world in which you live
and in the smallest corner of the heart
where truth is kept.
I wish you faith — to help define your living
and your life.
More I cannot wish you — except perhaps love —
to make all the rest worthwhile.

ROBERT A. WARD

22 Defeat may serve as well as victory
To shake the soul and let the glory out.
When the great oak is straining in the wind,
The boughs drink in new beauty and the trunk
Sends down a deeper root on the windward side.
Only the soul that knows the mighty grief
Can know the mighty rapture. Sorrows come
To stretch out spaces in the heart for joy.

EDWIN MARKHAM

23 Blessings we enjoy daily, and for the most of them,
because they be so common, men forget to pay their
praises. But let not us, because it is a sacrifice
so pleasing to Him who still protects us, and gives
us flowers and showers and meat and content.

IZAAK WALTON

24 Thou that hast given so much to me,
Give one thing more — a grateful heart;
Not thankful when it pleaseth me,
As if Thy blessings had spare days;
But such a heart, whose pulse may be
Thy praise.

GEORGE HERBERT

25 There is a rhythm in life, a certain beauty which
operates by a variation of lights and shadows,
happiness alternating with sorrow, content with
discontent, distilling in this process of contrast
a sense of satisfaction, of richness that can be
captured and pinned down only by those who
possess the gift of awareness.

LOUIS BROMFIELD

26 When you speak to people — smile. It is a wonderful
thing when you meet someone and they just instinctively
smile and say "I am mighty glad to know you."
There is power in a smile. It is one of the best
relaxation exercises of which I know.

HENRY MILLER

 **27** Hold fast your dreams!
Within your heart
Keep one still, secret spot
Where dreams may go,
And, sheltered so,
May thrive and grow
Where doubt and fear are not.
O keep a place apart,
Within your heart,
For little dreams to go!

LOUISE DRISCOLL

 28 Faith is not an easy virtue; but, in the broad
world of man's total voyage through time to eternity,
faith is not only a gracious companion,
but an essential guide.

THEODORE M. HESBURGH

 **29** It need not discourage us if we are full
of doubts. Healthy questions keep faith dynamic.
In fact, unless we start with doubts we cannot have
a deep-rooted faith. One who believes lightly and
unthinkingly has not much of a belief. He who has
a faith which is not to be shaken has won it through
blood and tears — has worked his way from doubt
to truth as one who reaches a clearing through
a thicket of brambles and thorns.

HELEN KELLER

30 It is only in exceptional moods that we realize how wonderful are the commonest experiences of life. It seems to me sometimes that these experiences have an "inner" side, as well as the outer side we normally perceive. At such moments one suddenly sees everything with new eyes; one feels on the brink of some great revelation. It is as if we caught a glimpse of some incredibly beautiful world that lies silently about us all the time.

J. W. N. SULLIVAN

DECEMBER

 1 You can always tell a real friend:
when you've made a fool of yourself he doesn't feel you've done a permanent job.

LAURENCE J. PETER

 2 Here is the secret of inspiration.
Tell yourself that thousands and tens of people, not very intelligent and certainly no more intelligent than the rest of us, have mastered problems as difficult as those
that now baffle you.

WILLIAM FEATHER

3 If the day and the night are such that you greet them with joy, and life emits a fragrance like flowers and sweet-scented herbs, is more elastic, more starry, more immortal, —
that is your success.

HENRY DAVID THOREAU

 **4**

To desire and strive to be of some service to the
world, to aim at doing something which shall really
increase the happiness and welfare and virtue of
mankind — this is a choice which is possible for all
of us; and surely it is a good haven to sail for.

HENRY VAN DYKE

 5

The wise man in the storm prays God, not for
safety from danger, but for deliverance from fear.
It is the storm within which endangers him, not
the storm without.

RALPH WALDO EMERSON

 6

Our abundant plains and mountains would yield little
if it were not for the applied skill and energy of
Americans working together as fellow citizens bound
up in common destiny. The achievement of
brotherhood is the crowning objective of our society.

DWIGHT D. EISENHOWER

 7

When an archer misses the mark he turns and
looks for the fault within himself. Failure to hit
the bull's-eye is never the fault of the target.
To improve your aim improve yourself.

GILBERT ARLAND

 8

The greatest works are done by the ones. —
The hundreds do not often do much — the companies
never; it is the units — the single individuals,
that are the power and the might. — Individual
effort is, after all, the grand thing. —

CHARLES HADDON SPURGEON

9 Undertake something that is difficult; it will do you good. Unless you try to do something beyond what you have already mastered, you will never grow.

RONALD E. OSBORN

 **10** I do not know why it is more cramping to the soul to possess things it does not need than merely to desire them. It is harder to get rid of what one possesses than not to desire what one has not got; the former is like losing a limb.

ST. AUGUSTINE

 **11** Half the joy of life is in little things taken on the run. Let us run if we must — even the sands do that — but let us keep our hearts young and our eyes open that nothing worth our while shall escape us. And everything is worth its while if we only grasp it and its significance.

VICTOR CHERBULIEZ

 **12** When nothing seems to help, I go and look at a stonecutter hammering away at his rock perhaps a hundred times without as much as a crack showing in it. Yet at the hundred and first blow it will split in two, and I know it was not that blow that did it — but all that had gone before.

JACOB RIIS

 **13** Friendship, peculiar boon of Heav'n,
The noble mind's delight and pride,
To men and angels only giv'n,
To all the lower world denied.

SAMUEL JOHNSON

 **14**
Always laugh when you can; it is cheap medicine.
Merriment is a philosophy not well understood.
It is the sunny side of existence.

LORD BYRON

 **15**
Clay is fashioned into vessels; it is on their empty
hollowness that their use depends. Doors and
windows are cut out to make a dwelling, and on the
empty space within, its use depends. Thus, while
the existence of things may be good, it is the non-
existence in them that makes them serviceable.

LAO TZU

 **16**
Great events, we often find,
On little things depend,
And very small beginnings
Have oft a mighty end.

AUTHOR UNKNOWN

 **17**
The great composer does not set to work because
he is inspired, but becomes inspired because he
is working. Beethoven, Wagner, Bach and Mozart
settled down day after day to the job in hand with
as much regularity as an accountant settles down
each day to his figures. They didn't waste time
waiting for an inspiration.

ERNEST NEWMAN

 **18**
If I were to prescribe one process in the training
of men which is fundamental to success in any
direction, it would be thoroughgoing training in the
habit of accurate observation. It is a habit which
every one of us should be seeking evermore
to perfect.

EUGENE G. GRACE

 **19** Old and new put their stamp on everything in nature. The snowflake that is now falling is marked by both; the present gives the motion and color to the flakes; antiquity its form and properties. All things wear a luster which is a gift of the present and a tarnish of time.

RALPH WALDO EMERSON

 **20** One hour of life, crowded to the full with glorious action, and filled with noble risks, is worth whole years of those mean observances of paltry decorum, in which men steal through existence, like sluggish waters through a marsh, without either honour or observation.

SIR WALTER SCOTT

 **21** A good idea that is not shared with others will gradually fade away and bear no fruit, but when it is shared it lives forever because it is passed on from one person to another and grows as it goes.

LOWELL FILLMORE

 **22** The turbulent billows of the fretful surface leave the deep parts of the ocean undisturbed; and to him who has a hold on vaster and more permanent realities, the hourly vicissitudes of his personal destiny seem relatively insignificant things. The really religious person is accordingly unshakable and full of equanimity and calmly ready for any duty that the day may bring forth.

WILLIAM JAMES

DECEMBER

 **23** If wrinkles must be written upon our brows, let them not be written upon the heart. The spirit should not grow old.

JAMES A. GARFIELD

 24 It is the sign of endless life, for its leaves are ever green. See how it points upward to heaven. Let this be called the tree of the Christ-child; gather about it, not in the wild wood, but in your own homes; there it will shelter no deed of blood, but loving gifts and rites of kindness.

ST. BONIFACE

 **25**
Love came down at Christmas,
Love all lovely, Love Divine;
Love was born at Christmas,
Star and Angels gave the sign.

CHRISTINA ROSSETTI

 **26** If, instead of a gem or even a flower, we could cast the gift of a lovely thought into the heart of a friend, that would be giving as angels give.

GEORGE MacDONALD

 **27** To carry feelings of childhood into the powers of manhood, to combine the child's sense of wonder and novelty with the appearances which every day for years has rendered familiar, this is the character and privilege of genius, and one of the marks which distinguish it from talent.

SAMUEL TAYLOR COLERIDGE

 **28**

The wisest man could ask no more of Fate
Than to be simple, modest, manly, true,
Safe from the many, honored by the few;
To count as naught in world, or church, or state;
But inwardly in secret to be great.

JAMES RUSSELL LOWELL

 **29**

Lord of the far horizons,
        Give us the eyes to see
Over the verge of the sundown
        The beauty that is to be.

BLISS CARMAN

 **30**

The joys and sorrows of others are ours as much
as theirs, and in proper time as we feel this and
learn to live so that the whole world shares the
life that flows through us, do our minds learn
the Secret of Peace.

ANNIE BESANT

 **31**

The Year is closed, the record made,
The last deed done, the last word said,
The memory alone remains
Of all its joys, its griefs, its gains.
And now with purpose full and clear,
We turn to meet another year.

ROBERT BROWNING

Acknowledgments

The editor and the publisher have made every effort to trace the ownership of all copyrighted material and to secure permission from copyright holders of such material. In the event of any question arising as to the use of any material the publisher and editor, while expressing regret for inadvertent error, will be pleased to make the necessary corrections in future printings. Thanks are due to the following authors, publishers, publications and agents for permission to use the material indicated.

RICHARD ARMOUR AND BRANDEN PRESS, for "Money" from *An Armoury Of Light Verse* by Richard Armour. Copyright © 1964 by Bruce Humphries, Inc.

DODD, MEAD AND COMPANY, INC., for "A Bit Of Green" by Grace Schauffler from *The Days We Celebrate* compiled by R. H. Schauffler. Copyright © 1940 by Robert Haven Schauffler.

KENNETH L. HOLLENBECK, D.D.S. for "Hold Fast Your Dreams" by Louise Driscoll from *A Treasury Of Contentment* compiled by Ralph L. Woods. Copyright © 1969 by Ralph L. Woods.

HOLT, RINEHART AND WINSTON, PUBLISHERS, for an excerpt from "A Shropshire Lad"—Authorized Edition—from *The Collected Poems Of A. E. Housman* by A. E. Housman. Copyright © 1939, 1940, © 1965 by Holt, Rinehart and Winston, copyright © 1967, 1968 by Robert E. Symons. British Commonwealth rights granted by The Society of Authors, Literary Representative of the Estate of A. E. Housman; and Jonathan Cape.

MACMILLAN PUBLISHING CO., INC., for "April" from *Collected Poems* by Sara Teasdale. Copyright © 1915 by Macmillan Publishing Co., Inc., renewed 1943 by Mamie T. Wheless; for an excerpt from *Memoirs Of Childhood And Youth* by Albert Schweitzer. Copyright © 1949 by Macmillan Publishing Co., Inc. Published in the United States by Macmillan Publishing Co., Inc., 1949. British Commonwealth rights granted by George Allen & Unwin (Publishers) Ltd.

THE CHRISTIAN SCIENCE MONITOR, for "The Wind" by Philip Lazarus from *The Christian Science Monitor* (August 17, 1978). Copyright © 1978 by The Christian Science Publishing Society.

JOHN MURRAY (PUBLISHERS) LTD., for an excerpt from *From A College Window* by A. C. Benson.

Edited by Patricia Dreier

Designed by Wulf Stapelfeldt

Type set in Souvenir Light